SUENO(S)
FOR ALEJANDRA

Robert Estep

*aha***dada**

books

tokyo / toronto

General Editor: Jesse Glass
Layout and design: Joe Zanghi, Printed Matter Press
Cover photo: Barbara Shreffler

editorial address:

3158 Bentworth Drive
Burlington, Ontario
Canada L7M-1M2

First Edition
Printed and Bound in Canada

ISBN 978-0-981244-0-9

*For my mother, Janina,
and in memory of my father, Hunter*

Acknowledgements:

Special thanks to Robert Gibbons and Susan Bassnett for support and commentary, and to Michelle Estep for proofing.

POEMS

DULCAMARA

In the out-of-doors puppet show
a monstrous sans-culotte butchers
a Swiss guardsman, making great sport
of sawing, snik snik, through the paper
neck, the resilience of wire tingling the
wooden teeth as the strings tighten and shiver.
The guardsman's blue wig falls off
but bounces on the dangle of a single thread
and the curtain comes down on a gasp
that turns into laughter and applause
as two pretty girls step out smiling
from behind the stage.

NU

The glass roof glistens with moisture,
and looking up, the children suffer
momentary blindness. The adults
shade their eyes against the gold and white,
a skating movement as individual drops
grope together and slide away
until the entire crystal shift is gone,
leaving the blue sky, blurred
and a little smudged where each pane
grooves the thin copper bars.
The sky stays blue through lunchtime,
and then the ocean wakes up,
the wind takes note, begins to shovel clouds
across the city's ceiling, from left to right,
the river unwinding at its usual pace,
but with a slower, heavier look,
as the color deepens, absorbing the sky.

CHENEVIERE

Thin is what her trailing shadow says
and goes on gesturing behind her back,
playing hide and seek with skirt
over her head, the small buttons
on her open vest as green as twilight,
sewn with black thread to a spider's knot.
Lost in thought she drags her knock-kneed
shadow behind her, the blades of the
overhead fan sing like locusts, the damp
curls at her neck ruffle in the pleasant breeze.
She's meandering the baptistery,
on her way back to the arcade,
its dreams of solvency in constant yield,
little loves contriving to divide the day,
a parcel of hours to keep the fox
in sausage, take pity on the chubby hen
struggling in the wind.

CHIPMUNK

The short man rides the rickety lift
with a sense of pride,
his soul like an accordion,
proving many things at once,
juggling danger with abstinence,
curiosity with a rubber stamp,
wallet fat with urgency and lust
like champagne gone quickly to his head.
He swallows down his taste for waif,
but stubs a finger in imaginary
contract and ends with half a chicken,
roast potatoes, and asparagus a la fascisti,
drizzled with a meander of sauce.
The dirt under her fingernails
worth a second glass of wine.

GAZON

The word he used was 'sleeve' she thinks,
but wood smoke burns her eyes
and so she coughs and flutters her fingers
like a doll, waiting for the rum to pop
her stuffed-up ears.
She asks for a repeat but this time
the word is 'scarf' and he fists
an invisible steering wheel,
grinning fake-mad, fake-scary,
'grrr, Bugati, grrr'.

GLICINA

'You're all being very unreasonable'
the mezzo soprano from Lisbon says
to the landlord in his lobby.
In stockinged feet, enveloped by a bear
of a fur coat, she's sad and whiny,
determined to have her way. 'How can I
rehearse for so few hours a day?
Which of the neighbors complained?
Tell me and I will speak with them myself.'
Every bit as determined, the stocky
landlord keeps quiet, shrugs his hands
deeper into the pockets of his overcoat.
The agreement they reach owes nothing
to the desire for harmony, much to the
draught in the hallway. Three hours
in the morning for Mozart and Puccini,
one hour in the evening for whatever's left.
But no piano. The landlord watches her
go up the stairs, barefoot and classy
in the coat she says was a gift from Moscow.
Which Moscow would that be, he thinks
but doesn't ask. If French
is the language in Heaven by day, come
nightfall the angels switch to Portuguese.

GUNMETAL

'They ran that way, towards the river ...
there were three of them, the tall one
was holding a bird beneath his jacket,
one could see its feathers, its feet
dangling down ... they were laughing
and one of them, the dirty-faced girl
with the black beret, was whistling 'Pistolero' ...
I yelled at them to slow down,
there's a trolley at that corner
and old folks, canes and impediments,
but they didn't stop and the littlest shrimp
had the nerve to call me a rude name.'

SUREAU

One end of the apartment block,
the one furthest from the river,
is still lit by gas lanterns,
ten feet above the street,
reached only by the man with the
Dutchman's pole.
The other end is a giant spider web
of electric string-lights, with
different-colored bulbs that make
each evening a holiday.
The authorities arrive at least once a week
to scold the disorder of the wires,
to prophesy a fiery death for those responsible.
And in the middle, like a medieval
throwback, drawn curtains flicker
and pulse with the glow of lit candles.
Séances, memorials, latch-key children
beginning their first love affairs.

EPSOM

A newsreel is being vetted
against the back wall
of the 'Marseilles' garage.
Cigarette smoke plumes
for a moment over white stone
then whirls, riding the draught
out the partly-raised grille,
spiraling up the streetlight
like Fantomas chasing the dragon.
The movie isn't much to look at
but it passes the time,
a pith helmet bobbing above fronds
in a hotel lobby, the ruins
of the old slave market,
Port Au Prince, where no one's
been, not even the older brother
who swears sadly that Marseilles
is still his first love and someday
he'll return. The others cough,
scrape their chairs on the cold
floor, looking dubious.

GRENADINE

The banker comes out of the maid's room
with a clothespin on his nose, mimicking an
adenoidal lion's grrrff and a canary's
coalmined peep, calling out
their names as his children run round him,
howling with laughter. His wife sips
from her Nagasaki teacup, shakes her head,
glances at the clock on the mantel, but smiles
with her eyes, as he sinks on all fours like a bear.

CELADON

She hates the sound of her own nagging
and so she holds her tongue, separating
the children with a single blow.
Her husband's bath has ceased to steam,
but he'll get no apologies when he arrives,
cabbage-head or chocolate bars or promises
of one last run the length of Portugal.
She breaks down and threatens to box somebody's,
anybody's ears but no one's listening,
not even the fat blue parrot shuffling
on his swing, humming to himself his
'charlie? charlie?'

SPARROW

Aucassin's the secretary of the chess club,
Nicolette's the Marshal of her skating class.
Together they've agreed to bait their bears
at lake's edge, to rummage through the
differences that split the playground along
uneasy lines.
He grudgingly holds her by the mitten
as she undoes her shiny skates,
and quizzes her on friction as a way
of gauging her distress.
She gilds her vowels and notes that
golden sounds blush his cheeks a wild
rose.
He holds her mitten like a wilted flower
and his anguish makes her want
to dance with joy.

SARCELLE

Who would fail to be moved by such
a voice, pure as starlight in the country,
and a bending tone that seemed to caress
each care away. The grocer, pocketing
his massive key-ring, takes a few steps
into the street and stops to listen.
Everything comes to an end, he knows,
he even understands, but that voice
could have gone on all night and he'd
not have grown tired of it.

BAMBU

Three years service in the East
and the new waiter lavishes each pair
of violet eyes with a mince and
elephant squat and tickles their Vermeer
ears with plagiaries of opium, kabuki,
and geisha, of rosewater snow-cones and
love at the foot of Mount Fuji,
while the saffron sun rose from the sea,
over a can-can of belching frogs
each the size of a Breton menhir.
—Good for business, winks the surly patron.

POLIGNAC

The straight-backed beauty chooses
symmetry over comfort, the train
either overdue or missed when she
was watching her reflection in the
mendicant drunkard's eyes. She gave
no cry of outrage or approval,
watching as the two policemen
beat him briefly and humped his albatross
to the darkened side of the tracks.
She rests her arms on the vintner's
abandoned sandwich board, clenching
her fists as the equal sign lights up.

PISSENLIT

During the last minutes of the
one hundred-year old Spring
someone leaves a guitar
in the back of a taxi and jumps the fare,
the vortex round the Place de la Concorde
having stalled just long enough
for fugitive instinct to override
sentiment, ears stopped
against the cries coming from
within the battered Braque-blue case.

CREAM

At a street corner the Basque's girlfriend
lets a stranger flick the foam from her chin,
anarchist's black settling its cape
over the arcade's breathing sky.
His homburg shadowing to the bridge
of his nose, 'Passagen' and another
foreign word that pinches her from
threat to comfort, the directions she will
give the same as she would give to any man.

CHALK

A razor strap hangs from the wall
and next to it a deflated bicycle tire,
stretched to obscene oval and nailed
crazy to a water stain that seems to pulse,
thanks to the drawn out death
of the lightbulb, sizzling and naked
and almost cheerful above the head
of the man who'll buy her breakfast.

TOURNESOL

The analyst's menu is red-lettered
on a beige card, a sliding scale for
traumas, with less glamorous quirks
discounted according to an
'embarrassment' factor.
Diagnosis is guaranteed or nearly,
some distant cure exuding like a pearl
to the pressure of cash and pills and tears.
Ice-water's back in fashion,
along with rubber pants and
jumper cables and the urchins
handing round the cards
couldn't read them if they tried.

BYZANCE

A girl spins round a copper pole,
her smile growing more fake
with each new pass of the compass-
points, her long legs, short hair, and
ivory gash made multiple in ceiling
mirrors and bloodshot eyes,
the 'oohs' when she goes up,
the 'aahs' when she comes down,
a sound like loose change on a marble
counter top, turning into rain.

SMOKE

An hour of accordion and orphan voice,
followed by guitar and Russian Orthodox
complaint, the barber up the hall shouting
turn that goddamned radio down
but everywhere there's someone listening
for the key to their next move,
the cryptic mix of bird and plaster
that will coax the landlord's daughter
to a lovestruck knickers-drop,
embezzlement the tidy topic when
pillow talk takes a practical turn.

ARDOISE

She connects the state of love
with the word 'Kandinsky'
but not with the word 'Miro'
and doesn't move beyond
awareness to analysis. Love, like
laziness, a great distraction to lose
oneself in, a happy loss, yes, and
somehow entwined with a palette
based on starvation in winter,
of the man who approached her
as a stranger two hours ago,
with whom she quietly negotiated
in the rain, fat drops sliding
from availability down to the
Basque word for postponement.

LAPIS

The girl lounging the accosted stairs
spares half a thought to her latest nickname,
but inactivity drains her and she'll puzzle
more productively on someone else's time.
'Keep the change' is worth a smile
and she pretends to pencil in this tick-
tock name among the purple regulars,
pretends she sees her cousin calling
to her from across the street.

PERDRIX

The municipality of mushrooms begins here,
at the unlit footbridge quietly waiting
out an idle afternoon. Once they've
assured themselves she's no thief,
the quayside booksellers let her browse
undisturbed, give her back precise,
polite, answers when she asks the less-
than-obvious. She may be off
by more than a decade but when she
points out the thin blue erection
of the caliph's fabled minaret,
the dustier of her fellow browsers
tug their scholars' beards and nod,
knowing she's looking at the same thing
as they are.

CITRON

The Greek madam is burning coffee,
rope, hair, and toast and lost in thought
among the yellow invoices, synonyms
that foreign curse words can't quite match.
From the table in her basement office
she can see the cat in one window, shoes
moving past the other, where the sill
meets the sidewalk, where strangers
congregate to shelter when it rains,
to drop their cigarettes, still burning
as they flutter at the screen.

CONFETTI

Death with His hard-on comes flying
off the screen to the delighted shrieks
of half the quartier, their mobby push
and roar in a mad rush for the door,
and the calming tuba of a neighborhood
festival, smoke from frying eels and red
flowers as abundant as violins.
In the flicker of the emptied theater
the heroine beseeches the balconies,
rescued in a storm of paper snow,
her yanqui eyes for Death alone to melt in.

IPOMOEA

A drag-show for pirates has been postered
in evenses on the long walk home.
Painted-on moustaches, matinee idol teeth,
eyes an arrested blue one couldn't find
in nature, leastways this side the Himalayas.
The wardrobe's not so costly that it won't
end up as cast-off souvenirs, flung to the
sailors at the loudest table, shaved, showered
and rancid for action.

REQUIN

Two ships have collided in a fjord up
north somewhere. It was night
and raining. Of course it was.
No one can be blamed. The priest
taps the bowl of his pipe on the edge of the table
before reading the rest of the story
to his attentive companions. A third ship
arrived in time to rescue 40 people.
A further 8 were missing, unaccounted for,
not among the shivering survivors.
The younger brother from the garage
across the street shakes a matchbox slowly,
opens it, carefully takes out one match
after another, eight in all, laying them
on the table. He runs his finger
in a slow circle, shaking his head,
imagining the deep cold sea
swallowing the deep black night.

LLOVIZNA

The boy Gerard is splashing
through the puddles cobble-
tupped in Rue Git-Le-Coeur,
avoiding the ones where he can see
reflected red, his Hermes-flight
in inadvertent stalk of Modi's widow;
Amedeo M., scarecrow painter of deluxe bodies,
whose ghost he'll one day grow up to play.
Her pale hands cup her threadbare elbows
as she somnambulates the black-as-oil street,
glancing up once to a high window
where she'll follow hope
right through the winter glass.

GUEULE-DE-LOUP

The prettiest one died less than a week ago.
Influenza, what else. The grocer frames
his gossip in question-and-answer form,
sliding the flat flask across the counter
as the priest unfolds his lonely bills.
The Jewish family that left last month
for New York or Philadelphia?
Replaced already, by some distant cousins
out of Trieste. Sure of that?
Yes, sure, and straight from the donkey's
mouth, just here for kerosene, absinthe,
and a bag of Turkish sweets.

SEVE

Sky tilts to accommodate the crane of spires,
youngest to tallest peering out across a plain
grown green. Barges line the river, the air
catches the bronze glint of refuse, someone
gobs from the belltower to the plaza below.

CAILLOU

Gerard's distracted aunt goes to slap him
for his soaking socks, but misses and
half-heartedly rearranges her birettes.
She knows better than to ask about school,
offering him the wooden spoon
fresh from the big red pot, asks him
instead about the one she refers to as
his playmate, the little soldier girl of the arcade.
He shrugs, licks the spoon, wants suddenly to cry.

CANNEBERGE

Nicolette is too afraid to recant,
seated opposite the principal,
whose bun was shaken loose
in the lunch hour tussle.
Which story will it be?
Either way she'll roast in the flames
of Hell Forever.
If the firemen stole the piano then why
did no one else see them push it
from the gym clear down the hall
and down the steps to the wagon
yawning at the gates.
Nicolette asks for the question again
at which the blond disheveled principal
releases a heaven-help-us,
rolls her eyes and, young enough
to be an older sister, sits back,
lights a cigarette and pouts,
red-cheeked and smiling.

ARBUSTE

She shows Gerard how to hold her,
slack, then firm, thumb making a figa
between his fingers to hook her skirtwaist
so she can lean out the 4th-story window,
spread her arms like Anais the trapeze artist
and catch the falling snowflakes on her tongue.
She laughs and tells him how cold it is
out here in the open air. With his knees
braced against the broken radiator,
the backs of her thighs pressed against his hips,
he feels the rivulets of sweat dampening his sweater.

SAUMATRE

Meanwhile, the taxi circles each monument
two or three times before joining one of the
streams of the pinwheel. The taxi stops
outside a bistro, the red banquettes
glowing softly through the frosted windows.
The blue silhouettes of the waiters and customers
waver on the glass. Sitting at the curb
the driver can make out neither type
nor nuance, and knows already
he won't find her again tonight.

MEDAILLE

The priest listens with one ear cocked
to the sound of rain on the canvas awning.
His retirement is less onerous than
he'd feared, amid his books and tobacco,
the lead soldiers he paints in the evening,
adhering to the historical accuracies
of the regimental trading cards.
Black boots, white trousers, green jackets,
the tiny dab to signify chevron,
blue for Austerlitz, silver for Marengo.
In twenty years' time he's brought an army
to life, displayed in bookcases backed by mirrors,
doubling the ranks, confounding the Emperor's enemies.
In the room next door are small boxes
filled with lead Russians, and Italians,
and Austrians. He wonders if
he'll live that long, to field them
in the honor that is their due.

CHERRY

Little soldier plants a kiss upon
the pony's velvet muzzle.
The trapeze artist moves about
inside the overheated tent, sits down
at a makeshift table, removes her
rainbow tights, lays out a hand of solitaire,
taps her forehead with a stolen
emery board, and asks what she will be
when she grows up.
Her voice is a sing-song chirp,
her accent from a farm that smells
like citrus in the summer.
Little soldier leans and plants a kiss
between the pony's velvet ears,
waiting for an offer before she answers.

SOUCI

Beside the bowl of yellow flowers the cat
advertises its orange qualities. Green eyes
never meet those of the pretty women
who peer in at him through the bright window.
He focuses on a space just above
their left shoulders, narrowing his eyes
to keep the light in tune.
The sun feels good on his coat.
He selects among the many sounds available,
allows the one which contains his name
to float against the glass, invisible between
the loud women and the admired silent bowl.

COLEOPTERE

On a traffic island close by the children's
zoo, a statue of a fairy en pointe.
Her toe on the pedestal then a perfect vertical
(the eye draws the line) to the tip of her finger,
pointing up to the sky. The ragman, already
drunk at noon, teeters on the corner,
his shoes rustling in the carpet of fallen leaves.
He smells himself, or the zoo behind him,
and feels ashamed, remembering that Christmas
morning years ago when he swears
the fairy came to life.

AZTECA

This end of the arcade is thick with
turpentine haze. Little soldier girl
walks in the dizzy light, starfish floating
under a sign for Bois de Chine.
A girl her own age, with a dirty jacket
and shoes too large, dances in the arcade's
echoing spillway. A man who might be
her father strums a brown and red guitar,
a lazy strumming that changes
to a hammering of notes and chords,
following close the girl's swoops and curtsies.
His smile turns on and off like an electric
light, the guitar fits into the curve
of his comforting arms like something
wild that he might tame.

AUTHOR'S NOTE

These poems arrived like fireflies in the middle of the day during a week in spring 2006. Their arrival was as unexpected as it was unbidden and I was too superstitious not to make them welcome. They settled in, six or seven at a time, one poem per page in the smallest notebook I have ever owned. 'Azteca', the first to be written, is now the last poem in the book, demoted in order to serve as a loop back to the beginning. I have not otherwise interfered in the order in which they were written.

Clearly a sequence from the start, I decided against my usual division by Roman numerals. The narrative line, light as it might seem, was one I felt could be safely intersected at any point and numbering the poems would have needlessly frozen them in place. What the poems needed were titles and titles, like typography, are of immense importance to me, frequently making themselves known before the lyric itself.

So I've given them colors.

And what, exactly, is the color of smoke? Like fire, it varies, depending on what is burning. And what then is the color of the word 'smoke'? No synesthetic sufferer shares their palette with a neighbor. The multiple answers to the question are those prompted by psychology and memory, and as prone to shifty renegotiation as time or mood.

These titles ('Smoke' included) are taken from the *Pantone Book of Color* (1990). Designed as a reference tool and organized in such a way that pleases both extremes of craftsmanship: strictness and precision or randomness and chance. Spend an hour going through its pages and patterns will emerge, guided by sound or shade or some personal arithmetical quirk likely to unravel if looked at too closely. Set the book aside and each repeat visit reveals new strands, sometimes echoing the earlier pattern but often as not brand new. Like picking apart the notes of a twenty minute raga, the time wasted or enjoyed is its own reward.

As for typography, I simply shook them free of their original paragraphs, defaulting to the two most pleasing models I know, and which I here happily acknowledge: the riddling snapshots of Jean Follain and the claustrophobic huddles of Cesar Vallejo's *Trilce*.

Forty titles, forty words, forty colors. Does it matter now that blue and its dilutions served as visual code for latch-key children, elementary truants, kids at the edge of the grown-up world? Or that green and its tribe were the lens filter for adult moments of vagrancy, paralysis, happiness, drift? After a week I had a pocketful of postcards, but not an atlas.

Will the Little Soldier Girl linger long enough to watch the dancing child curtsy and gather up the casual coins? Or will she ramble on through the arcade, arriving at an open-air puppet-show, to stand in the audience or sneak behind the screen as the Fall of the Bastille unfolds its carnage and comedy? Will the melancholy boy grow up to be the actor Gerard Philipe, who will one day play the role of Amedeo Modigliani in the film 'Montparnasse 19'? Will the neurotic taxi driver make one more circuit through the unanchored streets of his invented Paris and find the fare he thought was lost? I'm fairly certain that the atlas which holds the answers exists, but coaxing it into words is another job, for some other time, and maybe for some other writer. In the meantime it's enough that it hints from the blur of the margins, like H.A. Zo's illustrations for Raymond Roussel's *New Impressions of Africa*, pages left deliberately uncut along the top so that the reader sees what is visible without seeing all there is to see.

As to the title of the sequence. The poems are an unworthy tribute to Alejandra Pizarnik (1936-1972). Pizarnik, like so many young Argentine intellectuals and artists in the mid years of the 20th century, was drawn to Europe as a means of centering her art before relaunching herself back across the Atlantic. She spent time in Paris in the 1950s and suffered badly from homesickness, doubting her knowledge of French, doubting her talent as a poet, feeling surrounded by the loneliness of the ancient landmarks, and by the menace and seduction of the city's many ghosts. All of which she painfully and beautifully recorded in her diaries. She is, incidentally, one of the great explorers of shadows and their uncanny possibilities.

'Sueno' is, of course, the Spanish word for sleep, dream, nap, daydream. So, these poems are little daydreams from one poet to another, both lovers of Paris and all things French, but neither of us quite at home there.

About the Author

Robert Estep was born in 1956 in Washington, D.C. He attended the University of Texas at Austin, where he studied English and French literature. He has lived in Costa Rica, Venezuela, Chile, and Mexico City, and currently lives in Houston, Texas, where he works at Fondren Library, Rice University.

OTHER TITLES FROM AHADADA

Ahadada Books publishes poetry. Preserving the best of the small press tradition, we produce finely designed and crafted books in limited editions.

Bela Fawr's Cabaret (David Annwn)   978-0-9808873-2-7

Writes Gavin Selerie: "David Annwn's work drills deep into strata of myth and history,. exposing devices which resonate in new contexts. Faithful to the living moment, his poems dip, hover and dart through soundscapes rich with suggestion, rhythmically charged and etymologically playful. Formally adventurous and inviting disjunction, these texts retain a lyric coherence that powerfully renders layers of experience. The mode veers from jazzy to mystical, evoking in the reader both disturbance and content. *Bela Fawr's Cabaret* has this recognisable stamp: music and legend 'Knocked Abaht a Bit', mischievous humour yielding subtle insight."

Age of the Demon Tools (Mark Spitzer)   978-0-9808873-1-0

Writes Ed Sanders: "You have to slow down, and absorb calmly, the procession of gritty, pointillist gnarls of poesy that Mark Spitzer wittily weaves into his book. Just the title, *Age of the Demon Tools*, is so appropriate in this horrid age of inappropriate technology—you know, corruptly programmed voting machines, drones with missiles hovering above huts, and mind reading machines looming just a few years into the demon-tool future. When you do slow down, and tarry within Spitzer's neologism-packed litanies, you will find the footprints of bards such as Allen Ginsberg, whose tradition of embedding current events into the flow of poesy is one of the great beacons of the new century. This book is worth reading if only for the poem 'Unholy Millenial Litany' and its blastsome truths."

Sweet Potatoes (Lou Rowan)   978-0-9781414-5-5

Lou Rowan . . . is retired, in love and charged. He was raised by horse breeders and went to Harvard and thus possesses an outward polish. But he talks like a radical, his speech incongruous with his buttoned-down appearance. *Golden Handcuffs Review*, the local literary magazine that Rowan founded and edits, is much like the man himself: appealing and presentable on the outside, a bit wild and experimental at the core.

Deciduous Poems (David B. Axelrod)   978-0-9808873-0-3

Dr. David B. Axelrod has published hundreds of articles and poems as well as sixteen books of poetry. Among his many grants and awards, he is recipient of three Fulbright Awards including his being the first official Fulbright Poet-in-Residence in the People's Republic of China. He was featured in Newsday as a "Star in his academic galaxy," and characterized by the New York Times as "a treat." He has shared the stage with such notables as Louis Simpson, X. J. Kennedy, William Stafford, Robert Bly, Allen Ginsburg, David Ignatow and Galway Kinnell, in performance for the U.N., the American Library Association, the Struga Festival, and hundreds more schools and public events. His poetry has been translated into fourteen languages and he is a frequent and celebrated master teacher.

Late Poems of Lu You (Burton Watson)   978-0-9781414-9-3

Lu You (1125–1210) whose pen name was 'The Old Man Who Does as He Pleases,' was among the most prolific of Chinese poets, having left behind a collection of close to ten thousand poems as well as miscellaneous prose writings. His poetry, often characterized by an intense patriotism, is also notable for its recurrent expression of a carefree enjoyment of life. This volume consists of twenty-five of Burton Watson's new translations, plus Lu You's poems as they appear in the original, making this a perfect collection for the lay reader as well as for those with a mastery of Song dynasty Chinese.

www.ahadadabooks.com

Oulipoems (Philip Terry)   978-0-978-1414-2-4

Philip Terry was born in Belfast in 1962 and has been working with Oulipian and related writing practices for over twenty years. His lipogrammatic novel *The Book of Bachelors* (1999), was highly praised by the Oulipo: "Enormous rigour, great virtuosity—but that's the least of it." Currently he is Director of Creative Writing at the University of Essex, where he teaches a graduate course on the poetics of constraint. His work has been published in *Panurge, PN Review, Oasis, North American Review* and *Onedit,* and his books include the celebrated anthology of short stories *Ovid Metamorphosed* (2000) and *Fables of Aesop* (2006). His translation of Raymond Queneau's last book of poems, *Elementary Morality,* is forthcoming from Carcanet. *Oulipoems* is his first book of poetry.

The Impossibility of Dreams (David Axelrod)   978-0-9781414-3-1

Writes Louis Simpson: "Whether Axelrod is reliving a moment of pleasure, or a time of bitterness and pain, the truth of his poetry is like life itself compelling." Dr. David B. Axelrod has published hundreds of articles and poems as well as sixteen books of poetry. Among his many grants and awards, he is recipient of three Fulbright Awards including his being the first official Fulbright Poet-in-Residence in the People's Republic of China . He was featured in *Newsday* as a "Star in his academic galaxy," and characterized by the *New York Times* as "A Treat." His poetry has been translated into fourteen languages and he is a frequent and celebrated master teacher.

Now Showing (Jim Daniels)   0-9781414-1-5

Of Jim Daniels, the *Harvard Review* writes, "Although Daniels' verse is thematically dark, the energy and beauty of his language and his often brilliant use of irony affirm that a lighter side exists. This poet has already found his voice. And he speaks with that rare urgency that demands we listen." This is affirmed by Carol Muske, who identifies the "melancholy sweetness" running through these poems that identifies him as "a poet born to praise".

China Notes & The Treasures of Dunhuang (Jerome Rothenberg)   0-9732233-9-1

"*The China Notes* come from a trip in 2002 that brought us out as far as the Gobi Desert & allowed me to see some of the changes & continuities throughout the country. I was traveling with poet & scholar Wai-lim Yip & had a chance to read poetry in five or six cities & to observe things as part of an ongoing discourse with Wai-lim & others. The ancient beauty of some of what we saw played out against the theme park quality of other simulacra of the past....A sense of beckoning wilderness/wildness in a landscape already cut into to serve the human need for power & control." So Jerome Rothenberg describes the events behind the poems in this small volume—a continuation of his lifelong exploration of poetry and the search for a language to invoke the newness and strangeness both of what we observe and what we can imagine.

The Passion of Phineas Gage & Selected Poems (Jesse Glass)   0-9732233-8-3

The Passion of Phineas Gage & Selected Poems presents the best of Glass' experimental writing in a single volume. Glass' ground-breaking work has been hailed by poets as diverse as Jerome Rothenberg, William Bronk and Jim Daniels for its insight into human nature and its exploration of forms. Glass uses the tools of postmodernism: collaging, fragmentation, and Oulipo-like processes along with a keen understanding of poetic forms and traditions that stretches back to Beowulf and beyond. Moreover, Glass finds his subject matter in larger-than-life figures like Phineas Gage—the man whose life was changed in an instant when an iron bar was sent rocketing through his brain in a freak accident—as well as in ants processing up a wall in time to harpsichord music in order to steal salt crystals from the inner lip of a cowrie shell. The range and ambition of his work sets it apart. The product of over 30 years of engagement with the avant-garde, *The Passion of Phineas Gage & Selected Poems* is the work of a mature poet who continues to reinvent himself with every text he produces.

www.ahadadabooks.com

Send a request to be added to our mailing list:
http://www.ahadadabooks.com

Ahadada Books are available from these fine distributors:

Canada
Ahadada Books
3158 Bentworth Drive
Burlington, Ontario
Canada, L7M 1M2
Tel: (905) 617-7754
http://www.ahadadabooks.com/

United States of America
Small Press Distribution
1341 Seventh Street
Berkeley, CA
U.S.A. 94710-1409
Tel: (510) 524-1668
Fax: (510) 524-0852
http://www.spdbooks.org/

Europe
West House Books
40 Crescent Road
Nether Edge, Sheffield
United Kingdom S7 1HN
Tel: 0114-2586035
http://www.westhousebooks.co.uk/

Japan
Printed Matter Press
Yagi Bldg. 4F, 2-10-13 Shitaya,
Taito-ku, Tokyo
Japan 110-0004
Tel: 81-3-3876-8766
Fax: 81-3-3871-4964
http://www.printedmatterpress.com/